FASHION VICTIMS

FASHION VICTIMS
The Catty Catalogue of Stylish Casualties
From A to Z

Verse and Illustrations by Michael Roberts

COLLINS|DESIGN
An Imprint of HarperCollins*Publishers*

Fashion Victims: The Catty Catalogue of Stylish Casualties, From A to Z
Copyright © 2008 Michael Roberts

HarperCollins books may be purchased for educational, business, or sales
promotional use. For information, please write: Special Markets Department,
HarperCollins*Publishers*, 10 East 53rd Street, New York, NY 10022.

First published in 2008 by:
Collins Design
An Imprint of HarperCollins*Publishers*
10 East 53rd Street
New York, NY 10022
Tel: (212) 207-7000
Fax: (212) 207-7654
collinsdesign@harpercollins.com
www.harpercollins.com

Distributed throughout the world by:
HarperCollins*Publishers*
10 East 53rd Street
New York, NY 10022
Fax: (212) 207-7654

Library of Congress Cataloging-in-Publication Data

Roberts, Michael, 1947 Oct. 2-
Fashion victims : the catty catalogue of stylish casualties, from A to Z
/ text and illustrations by Michael Roberts.
p. cm.
ISBN 978-0-06-169538-4 (hardcover)
1. Fashion. 2. Clothing and dress. I. Title.

TT507.R627 2008
746.9'2--dc22

2008010875

Book design by Michael Roberts with Paul Lussier

Printed in China
First Printing, 2008

Dedication

This book is dedicated
To those who never rated
Each truly
Bad
New fashion
Fad
That should have been
Cremated.

And to Isabella Blow

Introduction

The Fashion World, it's often said,
Has wasted space inside its head.
And when it comes to introspection
Prefers a mirror for reflection.

But here, dear readers, we intend
To contemplate the world of trend.
Dissect the egos, greed, and lies
That dazzle fashion's butterflies.
And then in language full of sass
Strip bare the vain, the mean, the crass.

To show this can be swiftly said
We print it here from A to Zed.
And hope this proves a welcome guide
To fashion's excess far and wide—
Not just because it's most concise,
But 'cause it's cheap at twice the price!

a

Auctions

Diana's dress—it should be mine
In Flemish lace, it's *too* divine.
What's the reserve? Hmmm…pretty steep.
Darling—are you sound asleep?

Just look at this, it's *total* glamour—
Going soon under the hammer.
I know it's such a frightful slog—
But *please* peruse this catalogue.
You must admit she had great taste
A real celeb—God, what a *waste*!

Darling! Can you stop the snoring?
You always say these things are boring.
You make a fuss and say how tacky,
But look how much we made on Jackie!

I've marked the ones I must possess—
Ten suits, *five* coats, and this great dress.
I'll wear them once, then store them here—
The Beckham auction's due next year!

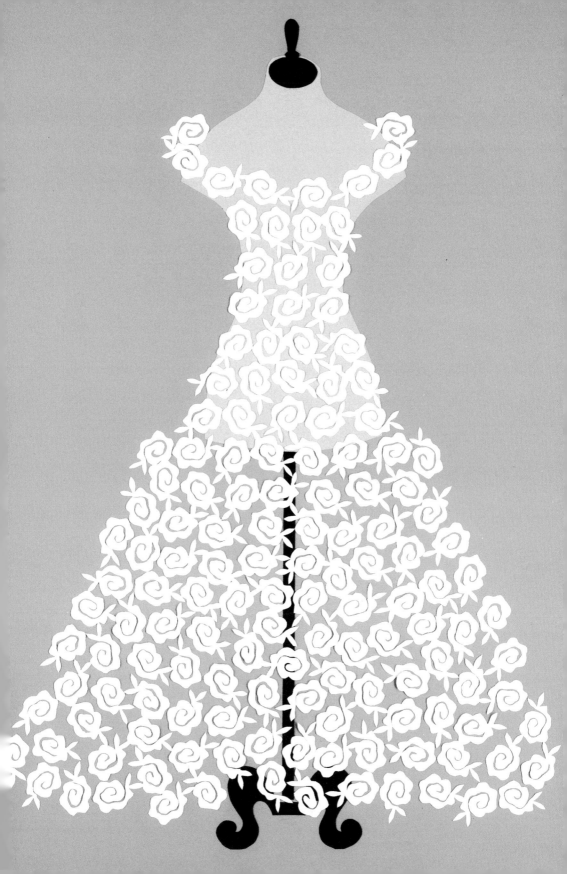

Bimbo

We go to parties, cameras pop.
I look really good, he feels on top.
I wear Alaïa short and tight—
He says it helps his appetite.

On opening nights, it's never boring
While he cuts deals, I stand adoring.
He calls me "Babe," I call him "Winner"
I'm always on his knee at dinner.
The flunkies bow, the waiters fawn—
They think I'm something big in porn.

He's buying Burbank—ain't life great?
(I love his choice of real estate.)
He told my agent I'll go far.
I'm thinking "Spielberg." Me—"the star!"

C

Catwalk

She's a disaster!
Can't walk at all.
Make her go faster!
Not very tall.

Why are her feet
So incredibly fat?
The face is no treat—
She'll need a big hat!

The hair is quite tragic
It's really a mess.
Not too much magic—
With her in that dress.

Try her in green—
Oooh—she looks like a stalk!
I'm going to scream!
Why *can't* she just walk?

How is her nose?
I *hardly* dare ask.
Do you suppose
We can give her a mask?

Designer

At six years old I dressed a doll in ribbons, lace, and flowers
My father said he wished me dead and made me take cold showers.

At twelve I took my mother off to buy the spring collections
Oh, what a waste of style and taste—she hated my selections.

At twenty-one, with childhood done, I studied hard at fashion
I sewed quite well, but truth to tell, fame was my guiding passion.
I learned to pose in outré clothes and clubbed till early morning
I slept in class, they kicked my ass—and threw me out for yawning.

I changed my name at twenty-five, became a good assistant
I worked all night, was bright, polite, and never too persistent.
I so disarmed with boyish charm, my hair as soft as sable
A hedge fund honcho came along and offered me a label!

At thirty-five, I felt alive, no one could stop me rising
They said my clothes were "quelque chose," "amusing," "smart," "surprising."

At forty-nine, my second line was priced at several billion
I lived in castles on the Rhine, my drug bills came to millions.
I wore a wig and Quaker clothes—my own unique aesthetic—
And never heard my workers say, "He's looking quite pathetic."

At sixty-one (which I'll remain for quite the longest time),
I fear the days are running out, but onward still I climb.
I diet, train, have sex again—I've scored some hunky catches.
But when I go, I'll go alone, with dolls and daddy's ashes.

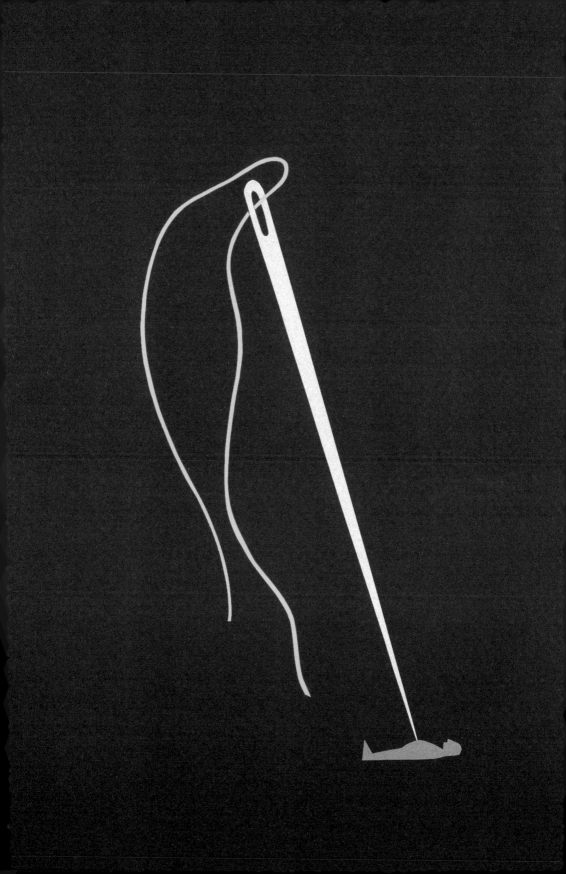

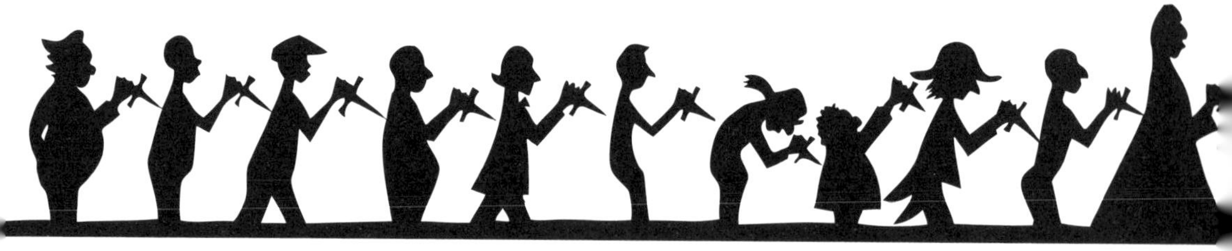

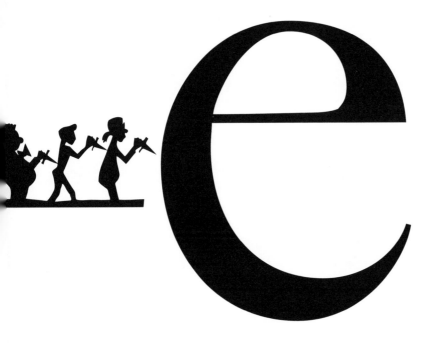

Editor

I am a famous fashion ed.
My branché style is très drop dead.
I'm awfully thin, but could be thinner
All this year I'm skipping dinner.

Karl has made me something new
The problem? Size. It's minus two!

I've reached the age where—I'm not blind—
A nip and tuck's not far behind—
And all the mirrors that I glimpse on
Give me hints of Wallis Simpson.

I do now wonder how to dress
I'm no spring chicken, I confess.
So do you think the way I am
Is much too "mutton dressed as lamb"?
Should my skirts be more discreet?
My hair more stately? Face more sweet?
Should my clothes be much less foxy?
Not so waisted, much more boxy?
Should I then be getting plump?

Oh, Jesus Christ—
I'm thinking "frump!"

f

Furs

Fran, while lunching, wrapped in sable,
Wasn't thrilled to flee her table.
When protesters shouted "Killer"
From behind a Doric pillar,
She felt sad and slightly hunted
As to a booth she quickly shunted.

Who, she wondered, have I harmed?
All my pelts were strictly farmed.
The minks, I'm sure, were in great shape
Before they lined my opera cape.
The marmot, wolf, and silver fox
Suffered few, if any, shocks.
And speaking of my shaved chinchilla—
Now it's hanging in the villa.
Surely, that's a happy fur—
It's resting on the Côte d'Azur!

Grooming

Brad, a model, shocked the nation
Showing off his depilation
As he stripped with great precision
On early morning television.

Off came the shirt, out came the pecs—
(He gave the screen a loving flex)—
As he explained in manner careless
How hot wax had made him hairless.

Viewers winced from Taos to Maine
As Brad displayed himself again,
And then described in graphic puns
Just how he got such silky buns!

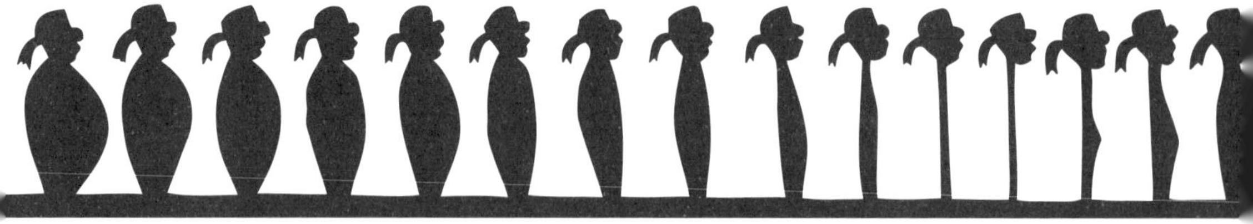

Heels

Bien sûr, I lurv to make les shoes
I lurv les teeny footsies
I 'ope ze penchant I don't lose
For torturing ze tootsies.

I make ze 'eels so very 'igh,
Les petites filles, zey tumble
But still zey pay to go zis way
It makes me very 'umble.

I don't know why I lurv ze cries
(I 'ave since I was seven)
Ze screams of pain now and again
Pour moi, it's perfect 'eaven.

Le crunch of bones on paving stones
Quelle joie de vivre I'm feeling!
But zey'll be back, it's just a crack
Zey lurv my sexual 'eeling.

C'est très, très chic, le pointy shoe
I cover wiz ze rosie
But footsies wide don't go inside
So chop off all ze toesy!

In-Crowd

Darling! *You*! How *are* you pet?
Have I seen you since the Met?
South Beach? No—last time I *cried*.
It's not the same since Gianni died.
You went to Cannes? My dear, *quelle* bore—
Without *one* interesting store.
Deeply tacky, La Croisette:
What you see *is* what you get.
Me? Oh nothing, *caro mío*.
Spring in Venice, fall in Río.
Went to Rome—Via Condotti.
Paris next—tea at the Lotti.
St. Tropez—stayed up too late
Bopping at Le Perroquet.
Saw Val and Carlos, Elton, too—
All were asking *where* were you?
Tried L.A.—had chat with Cher
(*Frightful* suite at the Bel Air)
Then back to Europe—*usual* plan—
Flew from Florence to Milan.
Got a lift on Calvin's plane—
Never doing that again!
He was rushing—*wouldn't* stop.
Can you *believe*? No time to *shop*!

Journalist

Alicia, fashion journalist,
Compiles her tabloid's "in/out" list
And dresses in the latest rage
As featured on her fashion page.
What others mock as simply vile,
To her is of the highest style.
And clothes fit for a rubbish heap
She finds "intriguing," "subtle," "deep."
Her wardrobe, vast and overflowing,
Has witnessed every gimmick going
From pointy bra to power shoulder,
The styles stay young but she grows older.

Come the days that make her sing
The Paris fashion shows for spring.
As hems shoot up and heels sink down
Alicia and her ilk hit town.
Like frisky fillies jumping fences
They frolic, filing *vast* expenses
Installed at Crillon, Meurice, Ritz
(whose service thrills them quite to bits)
They—between their bar selections—
Will take in just a few collections.

Poor Alicia, well she knows
That dreaded final day of shows.
'Tis when her small designer haul
She'll drag by bus to Charles de Gaulle,
And full of tales, some worth the telling,
Jet back to her suburban dwelling
Like all those girls of slender means
With hearts in France but homes in Queens.

NE
PAS
DERANGER

Kitsch

I do hate dressing like the crowd
I'd call my style unique
My mother thinks my clothes are loud
But she's some kind of freak.

The things I love are really neat
Like Seventies and plastic
And fluffy toys—they're really sweet
And Barbie—she's fantastic!

I'm very daring when I try
Bold colors for my makeup
My hair is full of so much dye
I'm blinded when I wake up!

My sister says I should be told
My lipstick's more than plenty
But that's because she's really old
I mean—she's almost twenty....

1

Logos

A society matron named Flo
Had a thing about labels that show
Then she read on the train
It was chic to be plain
Which dealt her a terrible blow.

Though she felt indescribably low
She preferred not to let it all go.
So she tattooed her frame
With every big name
From her waistband to just down below.

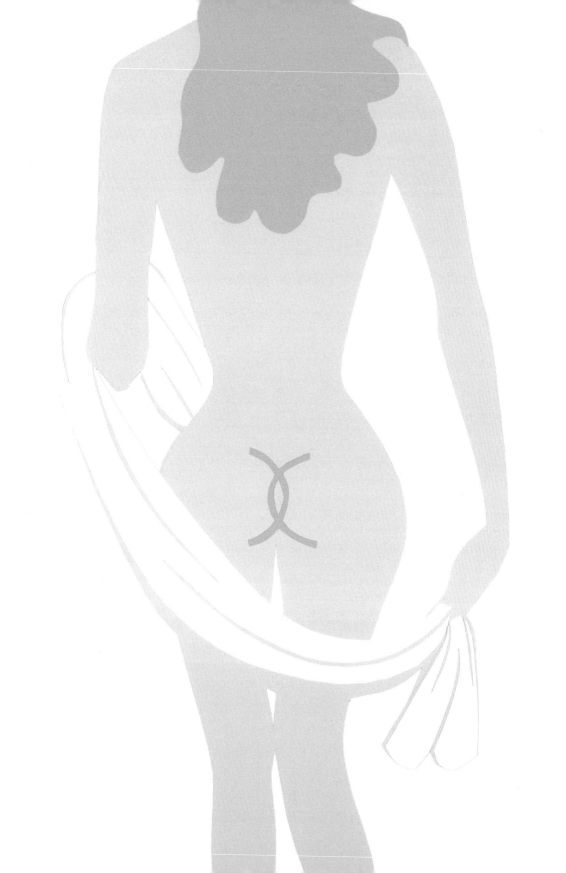

Model

My name is Trudi from Elite.
Like my nose, but *hate* my feet.
Modeling can be a drag,
And "go-sees" really aren't my bag.
But money's good, and that's a fact—
And socially my nights are *whack*!
London's such a trip, you know,
Always some cool place to go.
Concerts here and nightclubs there—
Never time to wash me hair.
My boyfriend deejays in a bar,
Saving up to buy a car.
Met Naomi at a gig—
She ignored me. What a pig!
Like my makeup?—It's real boss.
The earrings? Got them from Kate Moss.
Me and Kate—she's such a laugh—
Lets me crash out in her bath!
I really should keep off the booze—
This morning couldn't find my shoes.
I'm off to Thailand on a trip—
Phuket—is it really hip?
We're shooting *Vogue*—some beauty stuff.
Won't show my tits. *God, I look rough*!
Is that the time? Oh, shit. More troubles.
Still, I'm the star. I don't do doubles.

n

Novelty

Miranda was the techno type
She loved to shop online.
She bought it all—like half a mall—
And most of Calvin Klein.

Miranda was the try-it type
She bathed in mud at spas.
Used paraffin to clean her skin
And screwed her masseur, Lars.

Miranda was the social type
An "It" girl to the core.
Her e-mail mode went overload
With last demands from Dior.

Miranda was the reckless type
She never could say "when"
She dressed to kill on laundered bills:
She's doing eight to ten.

Opening

For Arabella, art-crowd maven,
Barrooms were the perfect haven.
Swathed in second-hand pashmina
(Now that times were getting leaner),
She sipped a drink both dark and mean
Far from the madding social scene.
Soon, she thought, without elation
I'll visit Damien's installation,
Drink cheap wine and nibble quiche,
Eavesdrop on the nouveau riche.
Flirt with dealers Prada-suited
Shaven-headed, Gucci-booted.
Idly chat with Wall Street traders,
Score some pot off corporate raiders.
I'll get so smashed, so paralytic,
I might throw up on some poor critic.
And if the evening gets too arty?
There's always Donatella's party….

p

Photographer

Why am I so fabulous?
What makes me truly great?
What would life be without me?
It's hard to contemplate.

No snaps of Brangelina or Paris hard at play,
No photo books of models' looks, their nipples on display,
No pages in the glossies of retouched wannabes,
No sexy ads in foreign mags to make you wish "Yes, please!"

No entourage, no autographs, no contracts by the score,
No makeup vans in sunny lands or studio hands galore,
No billboards straddling city streets with body parts gigantic,
Nor me with glass in premiere class crisscrossing the Atlantic.

So why am I so famous?
What makes me highly sought?
Let's call it art, but 'cause I'm smart
I'm happy to be bought.

q

Quality

Martha Stewart—can you help me?
I pick pine cones by the score
Want to make a nice arrangement
Hang it on the kitchen door.

Martha Stewart—am I hopeless?
My dried roses turn to dust
My meringues burn down to ashes
And my homemade loaves combust.

Martha Stewart—I'm appealing
Paper stars? Are they okay?
Henry stuck some on the ceiling
But they look a trifle gay.

Martha—you're my inspiration.
Made our home a work of art
Henry called it "a sensation"
Then he ran off with a tart.

Reviews

Lock the doors—it's Style dot com.
Timmy, dear—you must obey!
I need aromatherapy,
I had such vile reviews today.

Rip the mood boards off the wall
Throw the color charts away.
Burn the samples, trash them all
Look at what the papers say.

Yesterday I was divine!
When I commanded, they wore gray.
I cast my pearls before those swine
And now they say I'm "so passé."

Tear the patterns off their hooks
Not a pincushion can stay.
Leave my name to history books
I'll take the bonus severance pay.

S

Stores

It's not the fabric or the cut
That makes my clothes so dear,
It's when I rip the label out
That says "Made in Korea."

It's not the lining I admire
When I caress the collar,
It's when I rub the cost price off
And add another dollar.

It's not the happy shopping roar
That rouses tender feelings,
It's more the gratifying sight
Of suckers floor to ceiling.

Trends

I've tasted absinthe, done feng shui,
I've bought the bag by Vuitton, Louis.
My body fat's gone down the drain
I'm thinking Swedish pine again.
My scented candles smell of myrrh
I now wear feathers—never fur.
My blog's divine,
My script's just fine,
I won't do chat, except online.
I'm looking 'round for Mr. Right
with Jude Law's looks, but not his height.
I've sold an option on my book
How to Master Every Look.
I've dumped the boyfriend badly dressed—
(the one who called *me* self-obsessed).
Nothing much can get me down
A broken heel, the color brown
No upgrades on an L.A. trip,
A friend's success, a faulty zip
So as a rule I'm pretty happy….
Is this beluga? *God*, it's crappy!

UVA

My flip-flops match my bandeau top
Coordinates are "in."
Fluorescent prints with citrus hints
They complement my skin.
My abs are ripped, I've toned my hips,
My boobs were done last week.
I've had a perm, my butt is firm,
I made them peel each cheek.
When I awake, my protein shake
Is followed by a tonic,
Then endorphins and creatine,
Plus extra anabolic.
I use an aloe after-sun
Whenever I feel burning,
And on my pre-pilates run
I keep my pacer turning.
I like to skip, enhance my lips
With collagen injections.
My nails are frosted at the tips—
You've noticed the reflections?
My nose is fine (it isn't mine)
The Botox stopped my frowning.
And when I swim my plastic grin
Will sure prevent me drowning.

Valentine

Will I be your Valentine?
Depends if you've got sable,
I won't take fox
But love a box
With "ermine" on the label.

Will I be your Valentine?
Depends on what you offer,
I must be frank
I love a bank
But *hate* an empty coffer.

Will I be your Valentine?
Well, Tom and Dick and Harry,
I'd love to play
But first, you'll pay—
You've heard of "mercenary"?

Windows

They call me Pinkie, I'm a scream.
Here's my card, and there's my team.
At dressing windows I'm the champ
With staple gun and loads of camp.

My vast displays have shocked the city
I once used redwoods—*that* was pretty.
And when I put Lear jets in piles
The traffic stopped for miles and miles.

I can't do tame or understated
"Less is more"—I've always hated.
Which brings me to my new effect:
The work should whisper *intellect*.

The idea is—I love to share—
"Underworld Meets Underwear."
Get the picture? Cool Greek myth
Stretched from Madison to Fifth.

I'm thinking Hell—or more chic—Hades
Filled with pouting plaster ladies.
I'll do one window very crammed
With lost souls, corsets, and the damned.

Then Orpheus'll enter the hereafter
Dressed in naughty leather garters.
Here I'll put the River Styx—
I'll do it with some lighting tricks—
With Charon ferrying the dead
And tights displayed around his head.

Flames, I know, will be the issue,
But we can make them out of tissue.
Then neon lights will flash the story:
"Come Inside to Purgatory."

It makes me humble, gives me chills!
I feel like Cecil B. DeMille!
It's like *Inferno*—you know, Dante's,
But mine is bigger. And with panties!

X

Xmas

This time of year, I shed a tear
For melancholy peasants.
I feel so low
I have to go
And buy myself some presents.

I love to spend on all my friends
At least I do in theory.
But what I see
I buy for me
And feel so Christmas cheery.

You deck the halls with Christmas balls
It's oh-so-very-caring.
But most of all
When snowflakes fall
I just say "balls" to sharing.

y

Youth

Sarah's boyfriend—have you seen him?
Quite amazing, don't you think?
Heard she found him at Bar Pitti
Went and offered him a drink.

He moved into her apartment
Didn't really have a bean.
Story is he came from Aspen
Living off some frantic queen.

Now Sarah's bedroom's full of barbells,
Dirty sneakers, and old guitars.
Heard she sold the Francis Bacon
Just to buy him several cars.

Rumor is, he's bored already
Wants to work at VH1,
Tired of swanky uptown parties
Where they think that he's her son.

Sarah's grown quite fond of Xanax
So she's not that much *au fait*.
She'll be on her tenth Bellini
When he packs and moves away.

Z

Zips

Your hips so large
Are like a barge
That skirt you shouldn't try on.
You'll never fit
It's bound to split
Unless the zip's cast iron.

At summer sales
It sounds like hail
Your jacket buttons spraying.
We're crouching down
We've hit the ground
Dear zip, please grip, we're praying.

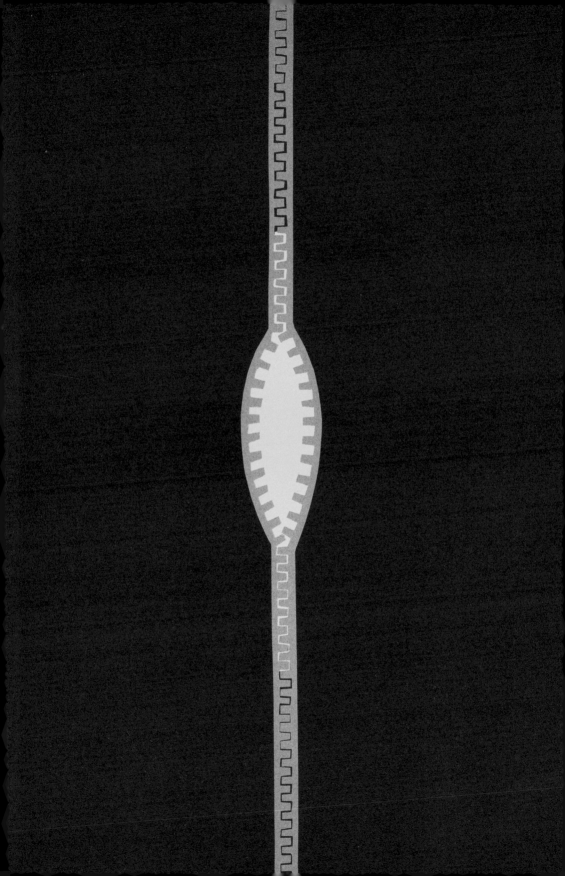

Acknowledgments

Paul Lussier
Diane von Furstenberg
Simon Doonan
Tim Blanks
Graydon Carter
Manolo Blahnik
Evangeline Blahnik
John Galliano
Diego Della Valle

David Kuhn
Geraldine Howie
Robin Howie
Tiggy Maconochie
Elizabeth Viscott Sullivan
Naomi Campbell
Jessica Diehl
Mario Testino
Giorgio Armani
Chris Garrett
Grace Coddington
Cathy Horyn
Noona Smith-Petersen
Véronique Plazolles
Amanda Harlech
Robert Forrest
Christopher Barnard
Elizabeth Saltzman Walker
Anne McNally
Karl Lagerfeld